The Trail
of Tears

The Trail of Tears

The Tragedy of the American Indians

KATIE MARSICO

Marshall Cavendish
Benchmark
New York

Marshall Cavendish Benchmark
99 White Plains Road
Tarrytown, NY 10591
www.marshallcavendish.us

Expert Reader: Michael Green, Professor, Department of History, University of
North Carolina, Chapel Hill

Library of Congress Cataloging-in-Publication Data

Marsico, Katie, 1980–
The trail of tears : the tragedy of the American Indians / by Katie Marsico.
p. cm. — (Perspectives on)
Includes bibliographical references and index.
Summary: Provides comprehensive information on the forced removal of
American Indians from their homes to the Oklahoma Territory and its
legacy—Provided by publisher.
ISBN 978-0-7614-4029-1
1. Trail of Tears, 1838–1839. 2. Cherokee Indians—Relocation. 3. Cherokee
Indians—Government relations. 4. Cherokee Indians—Social conditions. I. Title.
E99.C5M364 2010
973.04'9755—dc22
2008041217

Editor: Christine Florie
Publisher: Michelle Bisson
Art Director: Anahid Hamparian
Series Designer: Sonia Chaghatzbanian

Photo research by Marybeth Kavanagh

Cover photo by Jim Zuckerman/Alamy

The photographs in this book are used by permission and through the courtesy of:
Granger Collection: 15, 49, 72; Robert Lindneux, 2-3; *North Wind Picture Archives*: 8,
13, 18, 52, 60; *Getty Images*: Bridgeman Art Library, 12; Transcendental Graphics,
29; MPI, 36, 41, 64; Hulton, 78; Stephen Shugerman, 90; Brendan Smialowski/
AFP, 102; *The Image Works*: ANA, 22; *Corbis*: 67, 73; Smithsonian Institution, 28;
Bettmann, 86; Kevin Lamarque/Reuters, 94; *NativeStock*: 54; *AP Photo*: 69, 79;
USMC via National Archives, 82; Don Ryan, 93

Printed in Malaysia
1 3 5 6 4 2

Contents

Introduction

Like so many episodes in history that highlight the often unstable relations between American Indians and the United States of America, the Trail of Tears was an event that embodied intense emotions and undeniable realities. There was little question that, by the time the Cherokee Nation commenced its tragic journey in the spring of 1838, members of that tribe had already endured centuries of fighting to preserve their land rights and their way of life. There was also no doubt that U.S. citizens were anxious for their country to expand so that they could take advantage of bountiful farmland, lush forests, and the gold and minerals that made many Americans rich quickly. Regrettably, one of the ways they opted to accomplish this was by encroaching upon territory that already belonged to tribes such as the Cherokee.

Once the American Indians began their forced journey from the Southeast to their new homes in Indian Territory, people from Cherokee children to Christian missionaries to U.S. soldiers voiced their perspectives on the Trail of Tears, and their thoughts and remembrances continue to echo in the twenty-first century. Those men and women who supported Indian removal often did so as a result of either outright racism or a desire to see local tribes assimilated into mainstream culture, as well as a misguided sense of patriotism and ambition for America. Similarly, while some soldiers who shuttled the Cherokee westward were undeniably brutal and motivated by racial ignorance, others were often moved to pity, regret, and horror by the task with which they were charged and its impact on the people under their watch.

Yet what meaning does the Trail of Tears have for modern citizens of the Cherokee Nation and non-American Indians in the United States nearly two centuries later? How long did it take for relations to improve between the United States and the American Indians, and will there ever truly be a way to reconcile the two groups in regard to an event that resulted in the loss of approximately four thousand lives?

After considering the different perspectives of the cultures involved, it is important to evaluate the past and learn from it to prevent similar tragedies from being repeated. There is no sense or honor in pretending that the actions of the U.S. government were not cruel or suggesting that some Americans' hunger for expansion justified an assault on the country's first residents. Yet only by addressing sometimes conflicting vantage points will twenty-first-century citizens ever truly comprehend what the Cherokee experienced and why they experienced it.

Stated another way, it is essential to analyze the historical context surrounding the Trail of Tears and address the opinions and recollections of those affected and involved. This process of examining numerous perspectives is critical to enabling men and women of the modern world to take away some good from such a monumental tragedy in the form of greater cultural acceptance, respect, and understanding.

One

The Path Preceding the Trail

THE REVEREND DANIEL SABINE BUTRICK did not regard December 31, 1838, as a New Year's Eve filled with fond memories and lighthearted optimism in anticipation of the year ahead. Since the previous fall the minister had been in the company of a Cherokee detachment that departed Ross's Landing on the Tennessee River in what is present-day Chattanooga, Tennessee, and then made the subsequent trek westward to Indian Territory, in what later became the states of Kansas, Nebraska, and Oklahoma.

Under the supervision of white guards acting on the orders of the U.S. military, approximately one thousand Cherokee journeyed with Butrick. These men, women, and children represented but a fraction of their tribal brethren, who all had been forced to abandon their lands and lives in the southeastern states for an uncertain future in the West. Butrick used his journal to record the details of their travels along *Nunna ∂aul Tsuny* —"the trail where they cried" in the Cherokee language — more commonly known today as the Trail of Tears.

The forced removal of American Indians from their native lands by the U.S. government in 1838 and 1839 is known as the Trail of Tears.

9

"O what a year it has been," he noted on New Year's Eve in 1838.

> O what a sweeping wind has gone over and
> carried its thousands into the grave; while
> thousands of others have been tortured and
> scarcely survive, and the whole [Cherokee]
> nation comparatively thrown out of house
> and home during this most dreary winter.
> And why . . . what have they done to the
> United States. . . . For what crime . . . was
> this whole nation doomed to this perpetual
> death? This almost unheard of suffering?
> Simply because they would not agree to a
> principle, which would be at once death to
> their national existence. . . . This year has
> been a year of spiritual darkness. . . . A great
> part of the time my heart has been grieved
> to hear the awful profanements and see
> the scenes of wickedness which have been
> brought before us.

Yet such scenes of wickedness were not solely rooted in racism or hatred toward American Indians. White settlers and white politicians perceived Indian removal as a necessary step in the United States of America expanding its borders and taking advantage of the mining and forestry opportunities that existed on tribal lands. For the Cherokee and other American-Indian groups, however, this motivation was not sufficient to excuse being robbed of their lands and forced to participate in a mandatory westward journey. Their perspective differed greatly from that of the white U.S. citizens who eagerly eyed the Cherokee's former territories, but both groups would ultimately come to agree that the Trail of Tears was a historical event that forever altered lives and impacted the legacies of both the United States of America and the Cherokee Nation.

The Land and Legacy of the Principal People

The sorrowful scenes that Butrick recollected did not always define life for the Cherokee. Calling themselves Aniyunwiya, or the "principal people," they initially dwelled in portions of what are now West Virginia, Virginia, North Carolina, South Carolina, Georgia, Alabama, Tennessee, and Kentucky. As hunters, farmers, and gatherers, they gained sustenance from a variety of crops, including beans, corn, and squash, and hunted woodland animals such as deer, foxes, elks, rabbits, and bears.

The tribe was divided into seven clans, and each village was led by two separate political entities, the red government and the white government, which respectively maintained power in times of war and times of peace. Representatives of every clan met to discuss tribal affairs in seven-sided structures known as council houses. Various chiefs, priests, priestesses, counselors, and warriors played a role in the day-to-day civic and military affairs of individual Cherokee villages and of the Cherokee Nation as a whole.

European explorers first encountered the tribe in the mid-sixteenth century. Spanish conquistador Hernando

Many American-Indian tribes worked their land as farmers, growing a wide variety of crops.

de Soto crossed into their territory in his pursuit of gold, and they replenished his expedition with food and other supplies. Yet the amicable relations between the two parties were not indicative of all future interactions between Europeans and the Cherokee.

Hernando de Soto was greeted by American Indians during his exploration of the New World in the mid–1500s.

One of the Five Civilized Tribes

The Cherokee were regarded as one of the Five Civilized Tribes—a group that also consisted of the Chickasaw, Choctaw, Creek, and Seminole. These groups dwelled primarily in the southeastern United States prior to the Trail of Tears. They were regarded as cultured, or civilized, by white settlers because they gradually incorporated several European and American customs into their day-to-day existences after exposure to people who claimed those heritages. In addition, these Indians tended to maintain better relations with the whites who ventured into their territory than did other tribes in the area.

On the one hand the gold-hungry Spanish—and the English who followed them in the early 1600s—traded with the Cherokee for food items and provided the American Indians with iron, liquor, rifles, and gunpowder. For the first time ever members of the tribe laid their hands on innovations ranging from kettles to firearms, but they also were exposed to diseases such as mumps, measles, smallpox, and influenza. Faced with epidemics related to these new illnesses, the Cherokee population declined in number, dwindling from approximately 30,000 prior to the initial European contact to about 16,000 by the onset of the eighteenth century.

White settlers introduced several different diseases to the American Indians, greatly reducing their population.

Nor did armed conflicts with white emigrants bolster the population of American Indians residing in the Southeast. Even when the Cherokee were predisposed toward amicable relations with the settlers, Europeans recalled prior negative experiences with other North American tribes. Consequently, whites often assumed a hostile demeanor toward any Indians with whom they came into contact.

One Virginia colonist expressed this attitude in the mid–1600s when he and his fellow Englishmen discovered that a number of Cherokee had encamped at the James River near present-day Richmond, Virginia. The colonists had only recently finished battle with the Powhatan tribe and therefore stood determined "that these new come Indians be in no sort suffered to seat themselves there, or any place near us, it having cost so much blood to expel and extirpate those perfidious and treacherous Indians which were there formerly."

The "treacherous Indians," however, maintained a vastly different perspective. They witnessed white settlers engage in more and more frequent skirmishes with other local tribes, including the Creek, the Chickasaw, the Choctaw, and the Seminole. While some European colonists appeared eager to trade with American Indians for the food and other natural resources they needed to survive in a new land, they expressed an even greater greed for the land itself.

In an effort to hold on to the southeastern territories that had served as everything from hunting grounds to burial plots for their ancestors, the Cherokee even resorted to offering themselves up as allies to the whites during times of warfare. The tribe aided the colonists from 1711 to 1713 as the allies struggled to defeat their common foe, the Tuscarora, and again sided with British-American forces during the French and Indian War, which lasted from 1754 to 1763. Yet these temporary alliances proved largely fruitless for the Cherokee in the long term, and the tribe grew increasingly frustrated as the colonists set the terms for treaties that pushed the boundaries of white land ownership past the Appalachian Mountains and farther and farther west.

Both sides would periodically engage in skirmishes that involved Indian raids on colonial settlements and white retaliation that came in the form of settlers ransacking Cherokee villages. Ultimately, though, such bloody episodes generally concluded with another tense treaty that typically favored white land interests. The Cherokee begrudgingly accepted each new set of boundary specifications, because they were continually assured that it would be the final instance in which they would be required to cede additional territories. Regrettably, it never was, and the tribe subsequently turned to other allies in their struggle to keep their homes and their way of life.

"We had hoped the white men would not be willing to travel beyond the mountains," observed a Cherokee chief named Dragging Canoe in 1775. He continued,

> Now that hope is gone. They have passed
> the mountains and have settled upon
> Cherokee land. They wish to have that
> usurpation sanctioned by treaty. When that
> is gained, the same encroaching spirit will
> lead them upon other land of the Cherokees.
> New cessions will be asked. Finally the
> whole country, which the Cherokees and
> their fathers have so long occupied, will be

demanded, and the remnant of the . . . [Principal People], once so great and formidable, will be compelled to seek refuge in some distant wilderness. There they will be permitted to stay only a short while, until they again behold the advancing banners of the same greedy host. Not being able to point out any further retreat for the miserable Cherokees, the extinction of the whole race will be proclaimed.

U.S. troops destroyed American-Indian villages in the late 1700s.

Desperate to prevent fulfillment of this dire prophecy, the Cherokee fought with the British during part of the American Revolution (1776–1783) in exchange for the Europeans' assurance that they would in turn keep the colonists from further encroaching upon tribal lands. Colonial forces proved victorious, however, and the Cherokee lost nearly 10,000 additional square miles of territory by the time the conflict ended. With citizens of the newly formed United States bolder and more determined than ever to lay claim to southeastern lands, the tribe suddenly faced a government with which it would struggle for centuries to come.

Two Nations Within One Country

For the colonial champions—and even their forefathers, who had arrived in America a century earlier—the constant reevaluation of boundaries that divided their prospective territory from that of the American Indians was largely a matter of political calculation and necessity. Once the United States became an independent and globally recognized government entity, immigrants swarmed onto Atlantic shores, resulting in more than 5 million citizens claiming the United States as their home in 1800. All of these men and women needed land on which they could farm, open businesses and schools, and raise their families.

Though the Louisiana Purchase of 1803 nearly doubled the size of the nation by encompassing portions of Canada and fifteen present-day U.S. states, these geographic gains did not automatically result in amicable relations between whites and tribes such as the Cherokee. Dealings between American officials and European diplomats often failed to take American-Indian interests into account. Yet while the primary goal of the early U.S. administrations in regard to various Indian groups appeared to be to move tribes west of the Mississippi River, this was not the only consideration.

By the late 1780s the U.S. Constitution included articles that granted Congress and the president exclusive control over Indian affairs. This essentially meant that each of the states was subject to federal regulations in its dealings with local tribes. In other words white officials in Georgia couldn't simply buy Cherokee lands on a whim; any agreements between U.S. citizens and American Indians needed to be grounded in federal treaties.

U.S. Secretary of War Henry Knox was faced with the daunting task of forging policies that would allow for American expansion but that would simultaneously treat tribes such as the Cherokee as independent nations worthy of respect. Knox openly disapproved of treaties that U.S. officials had previously made with the Indians but had no intention of upholding in the long term. In his mind this type of diplomacy would only lead to expensive and unnecessary wars along the frontier, not to mention the ultimate extinction of tribal peoples.

On the other hand Knox also believed that the Cherokee and other Indians would have less friction with white settlers if the government took greater steps to "civilize" them. He thus orchestrated several treaties that included the following provision: "That the Cherokee nation may be led to a greater degree of civilization, and to become herdsmen and cultivators, instead of remaining a state of hunters, the United States will, from time to time, furnish gratuitously the said nation with useful implements of husbandry."

The decades that followed saw the U.S. government continuing to expand its borders at the cost of Indian territory, but officials also provided tribes with farm equipment and draft animals. The idea was to enable groups such as the Cherokee to rely on agriculture as a major source of commerce and to promote the creation of stable and permanent farms and villages. American politicians hoped this would lead to fewer skirmishes over land and would ideally make it easier for the Indians to live peacefully with whites who had already settled in their territory.

Missionaries and teachers also played a role in the government's efforts to bring "civilization" to tribal peoples. They gave willing Indians lessons in everything from Christianity to how to dress and cook according to the traditions and social standards of white American society. In turn some Cherokee embraced this new way of life and thrived because of it, raising cotton on large plantations worked by African-American slaves or running businesses in the southeastern portion of the United States.

But not every member of the tribe enjoyed this prosperous existence. Many Cherokee found themselves struggling to maintain a foothold on their territory and cultural traditions, which they would be forced to abandon in order to assimilate into white America. Several also had no desire to give up their ancient religious beliefs for the tenets of Christianity. These Cherokee realized, however, that there were certain benefits to maintaining varying levels of friendship with their white neighbors.

For example, the Cherokee continued to periodically side with whites during conflicts with other American-Indian

Missionaries played a great role in the effort to "civilize" American Indians.

nations, such as in the Creek War of 1813. These alliances occasionally served the Cherokee's own interests, if they themselves harbored feelings of hostility toward the enemy tribe in question. At the same time their partnership with U.S. citizens did little to protect their land rights. By 1819 the Cherokee had made twenty-five treaties with the settlers and yet maintained a mere 14 percent of their original territory.

Some members of the tribe recognized that it was point-less to resist and sold their land to white buyers. From the perspective of these Cherokee their hunting grounds had already been so severely depleted that it was useless to cling to woods and forests that yielded no food sources. Other American Indians, however, resorted to violence as they grew more desperate. The result was a series of attacks and counterattacks by Indians and white settlers on each other's respective communities. In the end, however, these incidents served only to bolster each side's misconceptions of and dis-like toward the other.

By the 1820s tensions had inched closer to a boiling point, as the U.S. government was adding more states to the Union at a steady pace. In 1824 American officials established the Bureau of Indian Affairs (BIA) to oversee all matters related to Indian land management and relations between the U.S. administration and various tribes. Yet this new government entity did little to improve life for the Cherokee, as they were routinely forced to choose between completely assimilating into white culture, moving farther west, or forever engaging in largely fruitless combat. But in dealing with the U.S. government, the Cherokee perceived the advantage of establishing a similar political infrastruc-ture for their own people.

In the mid-1820s the tribe therefore developed a con-stitution that provided for a two-body legislature, a court system, and a head chief to lead what the U.S. government came to acknowledge as the sovereign Cherokee Nation. The Cherokee declared its capital to be New Echota in Georgia, on the Oostanaula River. As a Cherokee named Sequoyah had established a written alphabet for his people

Another Look at New Echota

Early-nineteenth-century New Echota clearly challenged the misconception that all American Indians dwelled in tents amid an untamed wilderness. The one-time Cherokee capital was filled with well-kept frame homes, shops, schools staffed by Christian missionaries, a council house, a courthouse, a print shop, and farmsteads with fruit orchards, smokehouses, and barns. Today, New Echota is a state park and historic site and features several reconstructed buildings designed to capture the town's atmosphere during the 1820s.

in the early 1820s, it wasn't long before New Echota was the site of a printing press that published books and a newspaper called the *Cherokee Phoenix*.

Despite the fact that the Cherokee adapted to survive in areas that had once belonged exclusively to them but that had changed drastically over the course of a few centuries, they remained more steadfast than ever about certain issues. Specifically, as they agreed at a council meeting in New Echota in 1823, it was the "fixed and unalterable determination [of the Cherokee Nation] . . . never again to cede *one foot* more of land." Any violations of this decision were punishable by death. Unfortunately, the tribe would find it an almost constant challenge to uphold this vow in the years ahead.

Two

A Tragic Farewell to the East

In 1828 Andrew Jackson was elected president of the United States, a fact that promised little good for the Cherokee and other tribes that still maintained territory east of the Mississippi River. The president had previously fought alongside the Cherokee as a U.S. commander during the Creek War of 1813. Despite his comradeship with the tribe, however, the famously brazen and passionate Jackson rarely prioritized Cherokee interests over those of white settlers.

As he noted in a speech made in 1830,

> Philanthropy could not wish to see this continent restored to the conditions in which it was found by our forefathers. What good man would prefer a country covered with forests and ranged by a few thousand savages to our extensive republic, studded with cities, towns, and prosperous farms, embellished with all the improvements [that] art can devise or

industry execute, occupied by more than
12,000,000 happy people, and filled with
all the blessings of liberty, civilization,
and religion?

From Jackson's perspective, the nation that he had
been charged with leading could only stand to benefit
from westward expansion, even if it came at the expense
of tribes such as the Cherokee. His opinion was that the
Indians would be better off in western settlements des-
ignated by the U.S. government, where they would not
be constantly clashing with American citizens who were
determined to spread their civilization to the shores of
the Mississippi River and beyond. From the earliest days
of his presidency Jackson gained a reputation for ally-
ing himself with the state of Georgia in regard to land
disputes between white residents and members of the
Cherokee tribe.

While Georgians were anxious to purchase all Indian
territories that existed within state boundaries, U.S. policy
stipulated that such transactions could only be accomplished
by means of treaties with tribal leaders. The land could not
be taken by force, and the Cherokee firmly refused to sell
on a voluntary basis. Georgia politicians argued that they
should be able to wield state authority over the Cherokee
Nation rather than have to treat the tribe as a sovereign
entity that was not subject to state regulations. This would
essentially allow them to forcibly remove Indians who
inhabited areas that white settlers wanted to use for rural
and urban development.

As president of the United States Andrew Jackson supported the westward expansion of the nation, as well as the removal of American Indians west of the Mississippi River.

For his part Jackson believed that Georgia had a right to assert jurisdiction over any land within its borders. The president further argued that removal of the Cherokee would clearly benefit the tribe. No doubt, Jackson insisted, frontiersmen and the stark contrasts between white and Indian civilizations would ultimately bring about the decline of the Cherokee. Was it not better then to relocate them to the safety and solitude that existed west of the Mississippi River in areas that encompassed present-day Kansas, Nebraska, and Oklahoma? There, in what was referred to as "Indian Territory," the Indians' culture could flourish, and they could dwell in peace, without the fear of white encroachment and confrontation.

This trading card published in the late 1890s depicts a map of Indian Territory, a region west of the Mississippi River where various tribes were told they could live without interference from white settlers.

Jackson's intentions toward the Cherokee were made even more apparent when gold was discovered near Dahlonega, Georgia, in 1829. It didn't take long for settlers to swarm over the Cherokee town, raiding cattle and harassing the community. The disturbance to tribal life occurred a mere 70 miles from the Cherokee capital of New Echota and was troubling to the Indians for numerous reasons. Apart from the disruption and chaos the aggressive white presence wreaked, it was evidence of yet another broken treaty with the U.S. government.

In the late 1700s American officials had assured the Cherokee in a promise—which they had, in reality, already broken several times—that the tribe need not fear any further reduction of its territory. Complicating matters, however, was the fact that the government had guaranteed the state of Georgia in 1802 that it would eliminate any Indian land titles within Georgia's boundaries, thus allowing the state to further expand. Yet if federal politicians had initially hoped that the Cherokee would willingly sell their properties, they had since come to discover that the tribe was determined to maintain a firm grip on those territories it still retained in the Southeast.

Though the situation seemed at a standstill for a few decades, the discovery of gold in Dahlonega and Jackson's tendency to side with state interests and the needs of white settlers proved a critical turning point. To begin with, Georgia's officials, emboldened by the backing of the U.S. president, began authoring legislation that automatically annexed Cherokee territories to the state starting in June

1830 and prohibited anyone of Indian descent from giving testimony in trials that involved white defendants.

On a grander and more expansive scale, however, the federal government began contemplating a bill called the Indian Removal Act in late 1829. The proposed legislation was described as "an act to provide for an exchange of lands for the Indians residing in any of the states or territories and for their removal west of the river Mississippi." The thrust of this bill was the power it gave the president to forcibly relocate the Cherokee and other tribes from their homes east of the Mississippi River and transplant them to Indian Territory, which was largely unsettled.

The president and his supporters considered the proposal more than fair to all parties concerned. They argued that Congress would be allocated $500,000 for the purpose of compensating the various tribes that would be affected by the new law. In addition, proponents of the act noted that the Indians could, in fact, remain east of the Mississippi River — but they would have to agree to U.S. citizenship and would thus be subject to all the laws and decisions of the U.S. government rather than to individual tribal authorities.

At this time, however, Georgia officials — and arguably the president himself — had little interest in assimilating Indians into white society. From their perspectives even members of the Five Civilized Tribes, such as the Cherokee, would never measure up to the racial standards set forth by the white man. They might obey America's laws if they chose not to resettle across the Mississippi River, but they weren't capable of being reprogrammed in a way that would ever equal what so many Georgians and other U.S. citizens considered white superiority.

As for those Indians who opted for resettlement, Jackson and his supporters emphasized that they could maintain tribal sovereignty outside state boundaries and would not be restricted by the influence of white culture. The politicians even argued that, though the initial transition might be difficult, the Indians should regard the situation as one of opportunity rather than oppression.

"Our children by thousands yearly leave the land of their birth to seek new homes in distant regions," said Jackson. He continued,

> Can it be cruel in this government when, by events which it cannot control, the Indian is made discontented in his ancient home to purchase his lands, to give him a new and extensive territory, to pay the expense of his removal, and support him a year in his new abode? How many thousands of our own people would gladly embrace the opportunity of removing to the West on such conditions! If the offers made to the Indians were extended to them, they would be hailed with gratitude and joy.

Unsurprisingly, however, this is far from what the Cherokee and other southeastern tribes felt when the Indian Removal Act was signed into law on May 28, 1830.

Internal Strife and the Treaty of New Echota

In addition to the inevitable uproar the legislation fueled in tribal communities across the Southeast, even some whites—namely missionaries and U.S. congressmen from northeastern states—strongly disagreed with Jackson's policy. Massachusetts congressman Edward Everett warned,

> The evil . . . is enormous. . . . The inevit-
> able suffering [is] incalculable. Do not
> stain the fair fame of the country. . . .
> Nations of dependent Indians, against
> their will, under color of law, are driven
> from their homes into the wilderness.
> You cannot explain it; you cannot reason
> it away. . . . Our friends will view this
> measure with sorrow, and our enemies
> alone with joy. And we ourselves . . .
> when the interests and passions of the
> day are past, shall look back upon it,
> I fear, with self-reproach, and a regret
> as bitter as unavailing.

Many Cherokee were obviously inclined to agree with his sentiments, especially those who saw that the Indian Removal Act was essentially a mechanism by which the U.S. government could legally strip the tribe of its rightful property. The land in question was territory the Cherokee had claimed title to centuries before white settlers had even set foot on North American shores. And what of their new homes in Indian Territory for which Jackson expected them to express "gratitude and joy"?

"If the country to which we are directed to go is desirable," questioned Cherokee leader Major Ridge, "why is it so long a wilderness and a waste and uninhabited by respectable white people?" Despite Cherokee opinions regarding their futures west of the Mississippi River, however, it was obvious that officials in Georgia were determined to waste no time in using the Indian Removal Act to clear the way for white settlers' gold claims. Georgia governor George R. Gilmer quickly started parceling up Cherokee lands for sale and subsequently accused Indians who mined for gold on their own property of thievery against the state's white residents. After all, per federal law, Georgians were officially entitled to the property and any mineral rights that accompanied it.

The Cherokee reacted by appealing to the very government that had enacted legislation against them. Cherokee leaders pleaded their case to the U.S. Supreme Court, and Chief Justice John Marshall ruled in their favor in early 1832. He reaffirmed the sovereignty of the Cherokee Nation, stating that the tribe occupied a territory that "the citizens of Georgia have no right to enter, but with the assent of the Cherokees themselves." Widespread tribal exhilaration at this judgment was short-lived, however; President Jackson acknowledged the Supreme Court ruling but observed that Marshall and his supporters would be challenged in enforcing it. With southeastern settlers clamoring for land and gold and Georgia officials realizing the benefit of seeing their state boundaries expand, few whites in the region were overly eager to protect Indian land interests, regardless of Marshall's decisions back in Washington, D.C.

Perceiving the futility of gaining favor from the U.S. government when even Cherokee advocates within that body lacked the power to see favorable legislation enacted in the long term, some Indian leaders took another approach. The Treaty Party, which included prominent Cherokee such as Major Ridge, his son John, John Adair Bell, William Hicks, Elias Boudinot, Stand Watie, and Andrew Ross, believed that resisting removal was of no use. Better, they argued, that they push for a treaty with the American government that would afford the tribe the most sustainable existence possible, west of the Mississippi River.

Conversely, the National Party, led by Principal Chief John Ross (the brother of Andrew Ross), rallied the Cherokee to keep a tight grip on their territory. Ross frequently visited Washington, D.C., and pressed for the federal government to protect his people's claims in Georgia and other portions of the southeastern United States. Between 1832 and 1835 both the Treaty Party and the National Party became further divided, with each group holding its own council meetings and approaching U.S. officials with distinct policy proposals. Violence sometimes even erupted between proponents of the two factions, but it was the events of December 1835 that marked a climax in tensions.

While the majority of Cherokee council meetings had been relocated to Red Clay, Tennessee, after upheaval in Georgia in the wake of the passage of the Indian Removal

Cherokee chief John Ross urged the U.S. government not to force his people off their southeastern lands.

Act, New Echota was still the site of several important tribal policy discussions. In fact, New Echota was the location to which the U.S. War Department sent a representative named John F. Schermerhorn in 1835 to negotiate with the Treaty Party. The American government recognized its interactions with this group to be more productive than discussions with John Ross and his National Party, and it therefore collaborated with three hundred to four hundred Cherokee—including Major Ridge, Boudinot, Bell, Andrew Ross, and Stand Watie—in December.

John Ross, acting as an agent for the National Party, was occupied in Washington, D.C., and was unaware of the meeting in New Echota. The fateful decisions rendered there on December 29 would later shock him and countless other Cherokee to the core. Namely, the Treaty of New Echota explicitly stated that "The Cherokee nation hereby cede, relinquish, and convey to the United States all the lands owned, claimed or possessed by them east of the Mississippi River, and hereby release all their claims upon the United States for spoliations of every kind for and in consideration of the sum of five millions of dollars."

The tribe had two years from the date the treaty was ratified to abandon its territorial claims in the Southeast and set out for Indian Territory. The U.S. government assured the Indians that they would receive adequate means of transport and additional financial aid to enable them to survive during their first year in their new land. Alternately, those Cherokee who were against the removal could become U.S. citizens, subject to U.S. laws. These Indians would be provided with 160 acres of land in states where they already dwelled—not including Georgia.

A Sorrowful Conviction

Members of the Treaty Party were by no means overjoyed by their plan of action in late 1834. They nonetheless explained their rationale with the following resolution

> [The Treaty Party delegates] express . . . the sorrowful conviction that it is impossible for them, in the present state of things, to retain their national existence and to live in peace and comfort in their native region. They therefore have turned their eyes to the country west of the Mississippi . . . and they express the opinion that they are reduced to the alternative of . . . [migrating] to that region or of sinking into a condition but little, if at all, better than slavery.

Members of the Treaty Party had signed their names to the agreement in New Echota in an effort to help their people move on with their lives as quickly and easily as possible in light of what they considered inevitable white encroachment. Yet Ridge predicted that dire consequences would result from their diplomacy. Having been instrumental in drafting the treaty, upon affixing his name to the document, he prophesized, "I have signed my death warrant."

After the controversial gathering in New Echota became common knowledge, John Ross and thousands of his tribal brethren decried the proposed legislation. Along with approximately 16,000 other Cherokee, Ross signed his name to an official protest that was presented to Congress. Though their pleas fell on the deaf ears of the U.S. government, General John E. Wool, who was charged with disarming the tribe to prevent any type of military resistance, noted, "Many [Cherokee] have said they will die before they leave the country."

From the perspective of the citizens of Georgia and several American officials, the ratification of the Treaty of New Echota in May 1836 was not an act of cruelty. On the contrary, to politicians it was again a necessity that was critical to the growth of the nation. The Cherokee—and especially members of the National Party—obviously maintained a vastly different viewpoint, seeing the next two years as holding the promise of homelessness and hardship. Finally, the U.S. troops assigned to remove the tribe, which in 1835 consisted of about 16,500 Indians living east of the Mississippi River, prepared for the difficult and monumental undertaking, which was scheduled to commence in early 1838.

An Imposed Exodus

Since 1831 the U.S. government had been attempting to forcibly remove southeastern tribes such as the Choctaw, Creek, Chickasaw, and Seminole and relocate them west of the Mississippi River. Some groups didn't put up much of a physical struggle before they departed but nonetheless succumbed to diseases such as smallpox and dysentery, as well as to exposure to the elements. On the other hand, certain tribes such as the Seminole opposed the Indian Removal Act and its implications with armed resistance, which resulted in the Second Seminole War from 1835 to 1842. Ultimately, however, most of the Seminoles were either killed or captured and relocated.

By early 1837 the Cherokee Nation was essentially the last major southeastern tribe that American troops had not forcibly removed to Indian Territory. About five thousand Cherokee had already migrated to the opposite shores of the Mississippi River of their own accord during the previous two decades. On January 1, 1837, the first group of Cherokee to relocate under the provisions of the Indian Removal Act bid farewell to the Southeast. Approximately four hundred more Cherokee, including Ridge, his son, and Boudinot, made the journey before November 1837. Though a few fatalities were reported, the death statistics would in no way compare to those seen in the detachments that followed.

The remainder of Cherokee — most of whom were members of the National Party — stayed behind until the late spring of 1838, hopeful that John Ross's continued efforts in Washington, D.C., would spare them from forced removal. By May

The Seminole, who violently opposed the Indian Removal Act, surround a fort during the Second Seminole War.

1838, though, both U.S. troops and the remaining Cherokee, numbering between 14,000 and 14,500 Indians, faced the deadline for relocation set in the Treaty of New Echota.

Under the supervision of General Winfield Scott, the Cherokee removal was scheduled to utilize a variety of land and water routes. Those Indians being transported via water would travel along the Tennessee, Ohio, Mississippi, and Arkansas rivers. Scott and his staff arranged for Cherokee who would follow land routes to journey through central Tennessee, southwestern Kentucky, and southern Illinois, crossing the Mississippi River in Missouri, then progressing through that state and Arkansas to ultimately arrive in Indian Territory.

Before Scott could set this mass exodus in motion, however, he first had to round up thousands of Cherokee, most of whom had made no significant preparations for the relocation, because they still had faith that they would be spared from it. While he ordered the help of about two thousand armed soldiers to aid in this process, the general made clear his wishes—though they would not always be respected—that the collection of the Indians be undertaken with no unnecessary hostility or aggression on the part of U.S. troops. Scott likewise appealed to the Cherokee in a letter dated May 10, 1838, which addressed members of that tribe who remained in northern Georgia. He wrote,

> My troops already occupy many
> positions in the country that you are to
> abandon, and thousands and thousands
> are approaching from every quarter. All
> those troops, regular and militia, are your
> friends. Receive them and confide in
> them as such. Obey them when they tell
> you that you can remain no longer in this
> country. Soldiers are as kind-hearted as

brave, and the desire of every one of us is
to execute our painful duty in mercy. We
are commanded by the president to act
towards you in that spirit, and much is also
the wish of the whole people of America.
Chiefs, head-men, and warriors! Will you
then, by resistance, compel us to resort to
arms? God forbid! Or will you, by flight,
seek to hide yourselves in mountains and
forests, and thus oblige us to hunt you
down? Remember that, in pursuit, it may
be impossible to avoid conflicts. The blood
of the white man or the blood of the red
man may be spilt, and, if spilt, however
accidentally, it may be impossible for the
discreet and humane among you, or among
us, to prevent general war and carnage.

However pacific Scott's intentions might have been, the
Cherokee collection that was initiated in May 1838 was an
emotionally and physically brutal endeavor that took its
toll on Indians and U.S. soldiers alike. American troops
gave the Cherokee no notice as they rounded up the Indians with bayonets and rifles. The Indians had little time to
gather their belongings, many of which were subsequently
picked over by white scavengers, who helped themselves to
everything from livestock to cooking utensils.

An American-Indian boy named Samuel Cloud was barely
nine when he and his family were collected by American

forces. His remembrances were later transcribed by his great-great-grandson and include the following account of late spring 1838:

> It is spring. The leaves are on the trees. I am playing with my friends when white men in uniforms ride up to our home. My mother calls me. I can tell by her voice that something is wrong. Some of the men ride off. My mother tells me to gather my things, but the men don't allow us time to get anything. They enter our home and begin knocking over pottery and looking into everything. My mother and I are taken by several men to where their horses are and are held there at gun point. The men who rode off return with my father, Elijah. They have taken his rifle and he is walking toward us.
>
> I can feel his anger and frustration. There is nothing he can do. From my mother I feel fear. I am filled with fear, too. What is going on? I was just playing, but now my family and my friends' families are gathered together and told to walk at the point of a bayonet.
>
> We walk a long ways. My mother does not let me get far from her. My father is walking by the other men, talking in low, angry tones. The soldiers look weary, as though they'd rather be anywhere else but here.

They lead us to a stockade. They herd us into this pen like we are cattle. No one was given time to gather any possessions. The nights are still cold in the mountains, and we do not have enough blankets to go around. My mother holds me at night to keep me warm. That is the only time I feel safe. I feel her pull me to her tightly. I feel her warm breath in my hair. I feel her softness as I fall asleep at night.

Like Samuel Cloud the Indians swept up in the early stages of the removal process were temporarily housed in army stockades that were often infested with vermin and lacking in resources to meet the nutritional and sanitary needs of large groups of people. As a result diseases such as dysentery were common and caused the Cherokee death toll to rise even before some Indians had begun the trek west. These encampments were poorly equipped not simply because of the hard-heartedness of U.S. officials; the forced migration of thousands of Cherokee was a costly undertaking for the American government.

Scott and other organizers planned that the stockades ideally would be used only for temporary layovers, until the Indians could be moved to major points of emigration, from which they could begin their journeys westward. Such depots included Gunter's Landing in Guntersville, Alabama; Fort Cass in Charleston, Tennessee; and Ross's Landing. But what lay ahead for the Cherokee after being shuffled into stockades and then shuttled toward the western banks of the Mississippi River? What would it take to survive the

The Trail of Death from a Soldier's Perspective

Though the intense trials the Cherokee endured during Indian collection and along the Trail of Tears sometimes make it easy to assume that the U.S. troops who forced them westward were all hard-hearted military personnel, this was not universally the case. "I saw the helpless Cherokees arrested and dragged from their homes and driven at the bayonet point into the stockades," reported Private John G. Burnett of his experiences in 1838 and 1839. "And, in the chill of a drizzling rain on an October morning, I saw them loaded like cattle or sheep into 645 wagons and started toward the west. . . . The trail of the exiles was a trail of death. They had to sleep in the wagons and on the ground without fire. And I have known as many as twenty-two of them to die in one night of pneumonia due to ill treatment, cold, and exposure."

journey ahead and to coexist with white military forces over the journey's duration? More to the point, would the tribe's sacrifices and heartache—and unsurprisingly tenuous relationship with the United States of America—ultimately be worth a new life in Indian Territory?

Three

The Realities of a Rigorous Exodus

ONCE THE CHEROKEE WERE ON THE MOVE—initially ousted from Georgia and then from North Carolina, Tennessee, and Alabama a few weeks later—they were shepherded between stockades and emigration depots on their way westward. Those Indians forced to undergo a water voyage typically progressed toward Indian Territory via steamboat. A greater number of Cherokee traveled overland, however, and journeyed in wagons, on horseback, or on foot. For the most part U.S. troops reported the tribe to be generally cooperative, and several soldiers were not unmoved by the suffering they routinely witnessed. "I experienced no difficulty in getting them to move along, other than what arose from fatigue and this toughness of the roads over the mountains, which are the worst I ever saw," remarked Captain L.B. Webster in a letter to his wife in June 1838. "It was pitiful to behold the women and children, who suffered exceedingly—as they were obliged to walk, with the exception of the sick." Unsurprisingly, not every representative of the U.S. military was quite so candid in his observations. As rumors about the rigors of the journey and its toll on the

Those Cherokee who did not travel the Trail of Tears overland were sent west via steamboat.

Cherokee began to swirl, Scott responded by asserting to U.S. Secretary of War Joel R. Poinsett on July 27, 1838, that "The troops and Indians, in all their camps, continue to enjoy good general health."

This inaccuracy was published in several U.S. newspapers and served purposes that extended far beyond Scott's need for personal denial. From the perspective of average American citizens and distinguished politicians alike,

Origins of the Eastern Band

Not all Cherokee who refused to travel the Trail of Tears readily submitted to U.S. citizenship. Several hundred fled to the Great Smoky Mountains between North Carolina and Tennessee and continued to dwell in this region until 1842. The U.S. government subsequently allowed those Cherokee, whose descendants are now referred to as the Eastern Band, to settle on lands that now comprise the Qualla Reservation in western North Carolina.

the Indian Removal Act was not an exercise in cruelty ultimately designed to extinguish a race. In part, it was a massive effort toward U.S. expansion that cost money and was theoretically structured to be at least somewhat equitable to the Cherokee and other tribes. It followed that most people did not want to hear reports that the Indians were trudging through the mountains on foot and falling prey to everything from smallpox to physical exhaustion.

Nonetheless, such accounts continued to surface as the Cherokee made their way west. A missionary named Dr. Elizur Butler frequented the Indian camps and painted a grim portrait of life—and death—there when he shared his observations with a religious publication titled *Missionary Herald* in late 1838. "[Butler] writes . . . that the Cherokee were suffering severely from sickness," noted an article released in October of that year. "It was estimated by those having the best opportunity to judge that, 2,000 or more, out of 16,000, had died since they were taken from their homes to the camps in June last; that is one-eighth of the whole number in less than four months."

Regardless of Scott's optimistic assessments, Butler's were closer to reality. The majority of the Cherokee had been forced from their homes with little opportunity to pack or make provisions for transporting necessary foodstuffs and supplies. While it was true that U.S. troops provided the tribe with rations of flour, corn, bacon, and fodder for the Indians' horses, hunger was still prevalent. Those Cherokee lucky enough to have any weaponry in their possession—in light of the forced disarmament imposed by American soldiers and the rapidity with which Indian collection had occurred—hunted whenever opportunity allowed. Naturally, game obtained in this manner was hardly sufficient to feed an entire encampment, which usually consisted of about one thousand people.

In order to supplement the meager rations supplied by U.S. troops, some Cherokee left the Trail of Tears to hunt.

Rebecca Neugin, who was three at the time she and her family journeyed along the Trail of Tears, later recalled,

> The people got so tired of eating salt[ed] pork . . . that my father would walk through the woods as we traveled, hunting for turkeys and deer, which he brought into camp to feed us. Camp was usually made at some place where water was to be had, and, when we stopped and prepared to cook our food, other emigrants who had been driven from their homes without opportunity to secure cooking utensils came to our camp to use our pots and kettles. There was much sickness among the emigrants, and a great many little children died of whooping cough.

Though U.S. forces inoculated the Cherokee against certain diseases, such as smallpox, respiratory illnesses that ranged from the common cold to whooping cough, as well as physical exhaustion, dysentery, and exposure to the elements proved deadly. With the bulk of Cherokee detachments heading westward between the late spring of 1838 and the early spring of 1839, the Indians were faced with both scorching heat and bitter cold that were especially dangerous to the very young and the very old.

The Cruelest Work Ever Known

Those Cherokee who traveled by land covered an average of 10 miles per day, with some Indians even lacking shoes to protect their feet from rough terrain and brutal weather.

The Trail of Tears

In early January 1839 the *New York Observer* ran a telling article that included the testimony of a white traveler from Maine who crossed paths with members of the tribe who were journeying through Kentucky the previous December. "A great many ride on horseback, and multitudes go on foot," the witness recounted. "Even aged females, apparently nearly ready to drop into the grave, were traveling with heavy burdens attached to the back—on the sometimes frozen

Many Cherokee traveled by foot along the Trail of Tears during the harsh winter of 1838–1839.

ground and sometimes muddy streets, with no covering for the feet except what nature had given them."

The Cherokee who took a water route westward endured their share of hardships, as well. The rumble of the steam engines was a foreign and frightening sound to the Indians, and even more appalling was U.S. officers' treatment of those Cherokee passengers who died aboard ship. The tribe placed great importance in the religious practice of burying the dead in the earth, which made the soldiers' decision to lower the deceased into the water all the more mortifying. From the U.S. military's perspective, however, there was scarce time to pause after every mortality, go ashore, and allow passengers to commence rituals that most whites didn't full comprehend or appreciate. Nor was it sanitary to keep corpses onboard that had the potential to spread diseases to the living.

Estimates vary as to those Cherokee who failed to survive the Trail of Tears, but most historians agree that about four thousand perished along the way, falling prey to everything from starvation and exposure to the elements to diseases such as dysentery and respiratory ailments. There were also accounts of periodic skirmishes between U.S. troops and individual Cherokee that resulted in gunplay, which was alleged to have caused additional Indian fatalities. Regardless of the validity of these rumors, however, any Cherokee deaths that were the product of deliberate white aggression could not compare with the number of fatalities that arose from the sheer brutality of the journey westward.

Unfortunately, an accurate tally of deaths caused by the Indian Removal Act may never be realized, as records of

Every Possible Kindness

While episodes of U.S. soldiers antagonizing and assaulting the Cherokee under their supervision did undeniably occur, Scott issued an order in May 1838 that specifically prohibited such behavior.

> Every possible kindness, compatible with the necessity of removal must . . . be shown by the troops, and, if in the ranks, a despicable individual should be found capable of inflicting a wanton injury or insult on any Cherokee man, woman, or child, it is hereby made the special duty of the nearest good officer or man instantly to interpose and to seize and consign the guilty wretch to the severest penalty of the law.

those who perished were not kept. In addition, it is not unreasonable to assume that American commanders such as Scott had a vested interest in generating statistics that put as little emphasis as possible on the scores of Cherokee who didn't survive their forced exodus under the care of U.S. troops.

While fatality statistics may not be precise, the physical and psychological strain that defined the period from the late spring of 1838 to the early spring of 1839 is indisputable. On March 18, 1839, the final detachment of Cherokee—including John Ross—arrived in Indian Territory. The events leading up to that date had taken a tremendous toll on nearly every party involved, with one U.S. soldier remarking, "I fought through the Civil War and have seen men shot to pieces and slaughtered by thousands, but the Cherokee removal was the cruelest work I ever knew." With 1,200 miles of intense hardship behind them, the tribe was now faced with an even more intimidating task: reviving their culture to its former glory west of the Mississippi River.

Early Life in a New Land

Though five thousand Cherokee had already established themselves in Indian Territory before the passage of the Indian Removal Act, their reunion with members of the tribe who migrated west between 1838 and 1839 was not always joyous. On the contrary, different factions within the Cherokee Nation teetered on the brink of civil war as each attempted to maintain control of government affairs in their new land.

John Ross and the National Party had passed a resolution before the tribe began traveling the Trail of Tears that ensured their leadership policies would be followed in Indian Territory. This political maneuver, however, meant little to members of the Treaty Party and the Cherokee who had resided west of the Mississippi River for decades before the detachments of Indians arrived in 1838 and 1839. On June 22, 1839, tensions escalated into actual bloodshed when Ridge, his son John, and Boudinot were killed. John Ross was ultimately cleared of any role in the murders, but there was no doubt that the trio of Treaty Party leaders had been slaughtered for their policy making with U.S. officials in New Echota years earlier. Ridge's prediction that signing his name to the fateful treaty would be the equivalent of signing his own death warrant had proved accurate.

Nor were he and his comrades the only Cherokee casualties to occur west of the Mississippi River. Historians and anthropologists speculate that hundreds of Indians succumbed to the rigors of their journey after their arrival, as well as to the same diseases that had wreaked havoc on the tribe's population during the trek to Indian Territory. In addition, the Cherokee did not immediately flourish on their new lands. Many were impoverished and had been stripped bare of their most basic belongings when they were routed from their homes a year earlier.

"Very few of the Indians had been able to bring any of their household effects of kitchen utensils with them," an elderly Cherokee woman later recalled. "The old people who knew how made what they called dirt pots and dirt bowls. . . . In the same way they made dishes to eat out of, and then they made wooden spoons, and, for a number of years after we arrived, we had to use these crude utensils. . . . We had no shoes, and those that wore anything wore moccasins made out of deer hide, and the men wore leggings made of deer hide."

Clearly, the financial assistance promised by the U.S. government in the Treaty of New Echota was only a small amount of what the Cherokee needed in order to reconstruct their lives and culture. It was obvious that a strong tribal government was essential if they were to thrive in Indian Territory. To that end a new constitution was passed in late 1839 that made some strides toward unifying various Cherokee factions as the Cherokee Nation. John Ross was reelected principal chief and would retain that title for another twenty-seven years—until his death in 1866. The Cherokee then established their new capital in Tahlequah, amid the foothills of the Ozark Mountains in what is present-day Oklahoma.

Within a few years the tribe began making progress toward revitalization. Government buildings, businesses, charitable houses, and pastures and farmland started to take shape across Indian Territory, and white missionaries erected churches and schools. The Cherokee even breathed new life into their journalistic endeavors, printing a periodical known as the *Cherokee Advocate* starting in 1844.

Such efforts did not go unnoticed by whites who visited Indian Territory at about this time. U.S. soldier Ethan Allen Hitchcock noted in his journal during an 1841 visit how even those with Cherokee blood admitted that "The ancient customs of the nation are all gone." Hitchcock also added that "As we approached Tahlequah, we met several persons riding out, two women among them, well-dressed and covered with shawls, the men well-dressed with hats, and all . . . riding good horses. These people, said I, don't look very wild."

From the vantage point of the American government such an assessment was a clear indicator of the success of the Indian Removal Act. Not only had citizens in Georgia and other southeastern states prospered as a result of the legislation, but the Cherokee had managed to reestablish themselves farther west. A good number had even adopted

Some Cherokee began to abandon their native traditions and dressed in Western clothing after their arrival in Indian Territory.

certain aspects of American culture to replace what several whites considered a savage existence. From the perspective of the Cherokee the transitions of the 1830s and 1840s had not been easy but most members of the tribe had at least adapted to their new lands west of the Mississippi. It wasn't long, however, before both white citizens of the United States and Indians who belonged to the Cherokee Nation were thrust into conflict once more as cultures clashed, blood was spilled, and promises were broken yet again.

Four

Short-Lived Peace and Plenty

Beyond the great River Mississippi, where a part of your nation has gone, your Father has provided a country large enough for all of you, and he advises you to remove to it. There your white brothers will not trouble you; they will have no claim to the land, and you can live upon it, you and all your children, as long as the grass grows or the water runs, in peace and plenty. It will be yours forever.

So promised Andrew Jackson when he addressed the Cherokee early in his presidency, at least a decade before the tribe embarked on the Trail of Tears. For several years after they arrived in Indian Territory, it appeared that there was some measure of truth behind his vow.

Yet, just as the Cherokee had begun to reconstruct their lives, events rocked the United States that threatened to tear the nation apart. The Civil War raged from 1861 to 1865 over the much-debated issue of slavery, which, in turn, created division within the Cherokee Nation. Some Cherokee, many of whom were members of the old Treaty Party, still owned slaves and thus opted to side with the Confederacy.

John Ross, on the other hand, feared the implications of this alliance. His tribe lived on land that was in its possession as a direct result of treaties made with the United States. If the Cherokee alienated that sovereign power by pledging loyalty to the Southern forces that had broken from the Union, what would become of their claims within Indian Territory? Just as important, Ross and his constituents were concerned that the tribe had already assimilated far too much into American culture since the move westward. He therefore doubted the wisdom of the Cherokee embroiling themselves in what was regarded as a white man's war.

"The peculiar circumstances of their condition admonish the Cherokees to the exercise of prudence in regard to a state of affairs to the existence of which they have in no way contributed," observed Ross in a proclamation to the tribe in May 1861. "They should avoid the performance of any act or the adoption of any policy calculated to destroy or endanger their territorial and civil rights. . . . For these reasons I earnestly impress upon the Cherokee people the importance of non-interference in the affairs of the people of the States and the observance of unswerving neutrality between them."

Ultimately, though, the cries of those Cherokee eager to side with the Confederacy won out over Ross's pleas for neutrality. Confederate victories early in the war only bolstered the argument of those Indians who, rallied by former Treaty Party leader Stand Watie, believed that forming an alliance with non-Union forces was a prudent course of action. In the fall of 1861, despite the fact that a small fraction of Cherokee declared loyalty to the Union, the Cherokee Nation proclaimed its allegiance to the Confederacy. This led to about three thousand members of the tribe who had resettled in Indian Territory coming to the aid of Southern troops. By 1862, though, it was clear the action had been a grave mistake.

Union forces successfully occupied Tahlequah in the summer of that year, and Ross headed to Washington, D.C., in a desperate effort to gain President Abraham Lincoln's

During the Civil War a small number of Cherokee fought for the Union. This illustration depicts them at a Union encampment.

favor. Ross urged Lincoln to support and respect the treaties that had existed prior to the Cherokee Nation declaring allegiance to the Confederacy. The response of the U.S. government was to emancipate all slaves within the Cherokee Nation and to further reduce tribal lands within Indian Territory via new treaties created in 1866 and 1868.

The terms of these agreements were not designed simply to punish the Indians. Vindictive as they may have appeared to the Cherokee, the U.S. leaders who crafted the treaties were anxious to clear the land in question for railway construction and additional settlement. On the heels of a war that had essentially ripped the nation in two, it was more critical than ever that the United States experience growth and prosperity—both in actual size and in terms of connectedness that could be accomplished through building railroads that would ultimately crisscross the country.

Countless Indians who had not actively fought for the Confederacy nonetheless suffered due to the conflict. Hoping to escape the fighting that edged ever closer to tribal borders, thousands of Cherokee had sought refuge in Kansas, Texas, and Arkansas between 1861 and 1865. Many starved or perished due to exposure to the elements, with total death tolls as a result of the war climbing to more than four thousand.

The land on which the Cherokee had struggled to rebuild their lives after walking the Trail of Tears had been ravaged by combat and was gradually slipping away from the tribe's grasp as the United States and countless Indian nations entered into a new era of broken treaties and tense relations. The old dilemma of white Americans' desire for expansion versus the Cherokee's determination to survive would only become more complex during the final decades of the nineteenth century, when Indian Territory inched nearer to being incorporated into Oklahoma Territory and, ultimately, the state of Oklahoma.

The Dwindling Power of the Principal People

While the United States strove to renew a sense of unity and prosperity among all the states subsequent to the Civil War, the Cherokee appeared to have returned to the same poverty and degradation they had experienced in the late 1830s. Their lands in Indian Territory were largely war torn, and internal conflicts between various Cherokee political factions seemed to have flared once more.

As delegates from Washington, D.C., met with different tribal representatives, new treaties were negotiated, but the results of each were largely the same: the Cherokee had to grant rights-of-way to railroad companies planning to create transportation systems throughout their territory and also had to open up their land to other tribes that were being driven westward by the U.S. government. In 1866 the Cherokee agreed to sell portions of their property to the United States, including the Cherokee Strip—an area located along the southern border of present-day Kansas—and the Cherokee Outlet—more than 8 million acres of land situated in the northern portion of present-day Oklahoma.

Not only did the Cherokee desperately need the revenue generated by this transaction, but they were also anxious to be regarded as more than a mere ward of the U.S. government. They wished to be acknowledged as their own

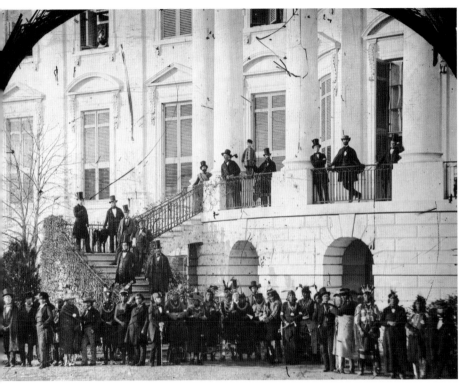

Tribal representatives meet with delegates at the White House to negotiate new treaties.

nation—which American officials promised would occur as a result of the sale. Being at a political disadvantage given their Confederate alliance during the Civil War, the Indians had no choice but to make some sacrifices to retain a measure of autonomy.

Though U.S. politicians agreed that the Cherokee Nation could maintain sovereignty, the concession held little weight. The American administration was eager to deal with all Indian tribes under the blanket of a single confederation that would

be overseen by white officials. The United States might therefore acknowledge the Cherokee Nation as a separate entity
unto itself, but it insisted on dealing with the all-encompassing
Indian confederation in any diplomatic endeavors.

Matters only deteriorated for the tribe in the years
that followed. In 1887 the Dawes Act was passed. This
legislation mandated individual ownership of lands that
had previously belonged to Indian tribes on a communal
basis. From the perspective of U.S. officials the process of
parceling off what was once tribal property was intended
to further assimilate Indians into American culture. Private
land ownership was more in keeping with the norms of
white society within the United States and would ultimately
serve to break the sense of tribal unity that so defined life
for groups such as the Cherokee.

In addition, the act enabled the U.S. government to hold
each land allotment in trust for twenty-five years, meaning
that it technically did not belong to the Indian property
owner in question until that span of time had passed. This
allowed white officials to redistribute land as they saw fit and
to parcel off any excess territory to white settlers anxious to
participate in westward expansion.

The Cherokee and other members of the Five Civilized Tribes were exempted from the Dawes Act until
1905, though the act itself remained in effect until 1934.
However, the U.S. government eventually convinced the
Cherokee to agree to the terms of the act.

Between 1887 and the early 1900s white politicians
continued their efforts to Americanize western Indians,
including the Cherokee. They also took steps that essentially

forced the tribe, which had been relatively unhassled by white intrusion immediately after its arrival in Indian Territory, to accept countless swarms of land-hungry white neighbors. September 1893 marked an infamous land rush in which approximately 100,000 settlers, also called boomers, awaited the sound of a cannon boom and then charged into the Cherokee Strip to stake property claims. The Cherokee had virtually no choice but to look on as Americans who did not share, understand, or respect their culture flooded into their lives and onto territory that had once been theirs.

Men on wagons wait for the official opening of the Oklahoma land rush in 1893.

Scores of Settlers and the Impact of Statehood

The men and women who poured into the western territories did not do so to deliberately antagonize Cherokee residents who dwelled nearby. The United States was suffering an economically depressed period, and westward-bound travelers were in search of fresh starts built on everything from mining gold to clearing farmland. For the Cherokee, however, the encroachment was a threat to everything the U.S. government had promised the Indians they would be protected from if they abandoned their claims in the Southeast.

Just as devastating to the tribe was the Curtis Act, which the U.S. government passed in 1898. This law essentially abolished tribal courts and placed all residents of Indian Territory under federal jurisdiction. Efforts to further diminish tribal authority began in 1907. As opposed to allowing the Cherokee to elect a principal chief, U.S. officials instead insisted that their government appoint one for the tribe. This custom would continue for nearly sixty-nine years, though some chiefs held office for terms as short as one day.

Thus stripped of many of the powers that had enabled them to survive even the Trail of Tears, the Cherokee ultimately agreed to land allotment in 1905. Under the terms of the Dawes Act each Cherokee family received 40 to 160 acres of land, which basically left 90,000 Indians of various tribes without property and deprived the Indian groups of 90 million acres of territory by 1934. Cherokee men were forced to work fields that were not readily yielding, and their wives were relegated to the household sphere, similar to the majority of white women in the early 1900s.

Yet Another Push for Allotment

Starting in 1898, U.S. officials instructed any members of the Five Civilized Tribes who were interested in being allotted land under the provisions of the Dawes Act to apply to the Dawes Rolls. The rolls were used to determine whether American Indians were eligible for an allotment based on their tribal status. Individuals were ranked according to whether they were tribal citizens by blood or marriage. People who offered other proof of ancestry were also considered, including African Americans who claimed Cherokee heritage based on their former affiliation with the Indians as their slaves.

Between 1898 and 1914 more than 101,000 members of the Five Civilized Tribes were listed on the rolls. Many Indians refused to apply, however, as they deeply resented the U.S. government by that point and opposed the fundamental principles of the Dawes Act.

The terms of the Dawes Act gave each Cherokee between 40 and 160 acres of land, though much of it unsuitable for farming.

From the vantage point of white onlookers, the Dawes Act and similar legislation that had squelched tribal authority had been a success. It had provided U.S. citizens with vast tracts of land in the West, which was critical in an era when homesteaders and participants in the gold rush raced across the Mississippi River in record numbers. In addition, it had further assimilated the Cherokee and other tribes into white culture. To the average white man the U.S. government had done the Indians a favor and had simultaneously enabled the country to prosper. As a Quaker philanthropist named Philip Garret wrote in the late 1800s, "Let [the Indian] lay side his picturesque blankets and moccasins, and, clad in the panoply of American citizenship, seek his chances of fortune or loss in the stern battle of life with the Aryan races."

Most Cherokee obviously maintained a different view of the situation. For them the lengthy struggles they had faced prior to and during the Trail of Tears had culminated in the near decimation of their culture and drastic changes in treaties that subsequently impacted their lifestyle and land rights. When Oklahoma was admitted to the Union as a state in 1907, the Cherokee automatically became U.S. citizens. By the strokes of a few pens in Washington, D.C., all members

Some whites viewed the Dawes Act as a means for American Indians, such as those shown here in Western dress, to assimilate into white culture.

of the tribe were suddenly part of a nation with which they had previously experienced largely strained relations. In addition, the Cherokee were essentially without their own country for the first time in centuries. All of what was previously Indian Territory was now part of Oklahoma and the United States.

It was a harsh blow for the Cherokee to sustain, but the events leading up to the early 1900s still did not deprive the tribe of its sense of cultural identity and purpose. As a famous Cherokee religious leader named Redbird Smith stated during this era,

> I have always believed that the Great
> Creator had a great design for my people,
> the Cherokees. I have been taught that
> from my childhood up, and now, in my
> mature manhood, I recognize it as a great
> truth. Our forces have been dissipated by the
> external forces, perhaps it has been just . . .
> training, but we must now get together as a
> race and render our contribution to mankind.
> We are endowed with intelligence, we
> are industrious, we are loyal, and we are
> spiritual, but we are overlooking the
> Cherokee mission on earth, for no man nor
> race is endowed with these qualifications
> without a designed purpose. . . . Our pride in
> our ancestral heritage is our great incentive
> for handing something worthwhile to our
> posterity. It is this pride in ancestry that

makes men strong and loyal for their principal
in life. It is this same pride that makes men
give up their all for their government.

Unsurprisingly, it was this pride that also enabled the
tribe to experience revitalization once again in the century
that followed, as well as to garner the respect of the U.S.
citizens who had become their countrymen.

Five

Seeking Rebirth in the Twentieth Century

DESPITE SMITH'S HOPEFUL PROMISE to his people, it was clear that the years immediately following Oklahoma statehood would not be easy ones for the Cherokee. U.S. officials were still unable to empathize on a level that would assure a better life for the Indians that did not involve complete assimilation into American culture. The United States had all but dissolved the Cherokee Nation, and its members watched as many of their former government buildings and educational institutions in Tahlequah were taken over by the state.

Unlike members of other tribes who ultimately forged their existences on reservations, citizens of the Cherokee Nation continued living in the same general area of Oklahoma as white residents who dwelled within state boundaries. Sadly, Indians were not always able to take advantage of the same opportunities as Caucasians in the early 1900s. Few had the resources to provide their children with a quality education or even routine medical care. American politicians were convinced the Cherokee were receiving adequate sustenance via aid provided by the BIA, while the Indians were somewhat limited in improving their own circumstances independently, especially in light of the powers that had been stripped away from their tribal government.

The Cherokee were technically answerable to U.S. laws and were due many of the same basic rights as average U.S. citizens, but the American government did little to help the tribe maintain its own cultural identity within mainstream society. Officials expected the Cherokee to assimilate into Caucasian culture and didn't offer much sympathy or assistance to those Indians who failed to live up to their expectations.

By the early 1930s the United States was in the grips of the economic crisis that became known as the Great Depression, and the Cherokee were not unaffected. Due to the Dawes Act and Oklahoma statehood, few members of the tribe had been left with land claims within what was formerly Indian Territory. Several of those Indians who had previously owned property had quickly become impoverished and had been forced to sell it and migrate to other areas, including California. In a bitter twist of fate it was often later discovered that their land was rich in oil prospects, which, in turn, padded the pockets of the white proprietors who had assumed control of it.

Though prospects appeared bleak for the Cherokee at this point in history, gradual changes began to make Smith's prophecy seem more viable starting in the mid-1930s. U.S. officials passed the Indian Reorganization Act of 1934, also referred to as the Wheeler-Howard Act, or the Indian New Deal. This legislation did much to

The Great Depression deeply affected the Cherokee and forced many, such as the family shown here, to migrate farther west.

reverse the impact of the Dawes Act by restoring tribal land claims, which replaced the privatized titles that had originally been forced upon the Cherokee and other Indians. In addition, tribes were allowed greater measures of self-government once more, as well as independent management of their land.

Secretary of the Interior Harold Ickes signs the Wheeler-Howard Act, which reinstated Indian self-rule.

Naturally, white lumbermen and ranchers voiced strong opposition to the act, which promised to deprive them of acreage rich in forests and grasses ideal for grazing cattle, horses, and sheep. Yet the U.S. Commissioner of Indian Affairs, John Collier, stood firm. Having visited a Pueblo village in New Mexico in 1920, he was so impressed with the self-sufficiency and harmony of the tribe that he was determined to restore the same lifestyle to other Indian groups who had been robbed of it over the course of several generations.

An article that ran in *Time* Magazine in February 1945 estimated that, thanks to Collier's efforts, the Indian Reorganization Act increased Indians' income by 300 percent and decreased their mortality rate from 28 per 1,000 in 1928 to 13.5 per 1,000 in 1945. The article also quoted Collier as saying, "The main thing now is that at least they have a will to live." For the Cherokee this will to live would soon intermingle with the realization that they could participate, prosper, and show patriotism within the spheres of both the Cherokee Nation and the United States of America.

Both U.S. Patriots and Cultural Preservationists

When America entered World War II shortly after the bombing of Pearl Harbor, Hawaii, in December 1941, the country needed to draw upon all its resources—in terms of both industrial resources and military personnel who could serve overseas—to combat the forces of Japan, Germany, and Italy. While the Cherokee and other tribes may have been initially unenthusiastic about being proclaimed U.S. citizens, the epithet nonetheless inspired a sense of patriotism over the course of several decades. Just as the Cherokee had perceived a threat to their survival during the Civil War, so did they comprehend the need to defend the country into which they had been forcibly incorporated when Oklahoma became a state. Hence, they and tens of thousands of other American Indians joined U.S. military forces during the course of World War II.

Many historians regard the conflict as a turning point for both whites and Indians. From the Caucasian perspective World War II helped various tribes further assimilate into white society—a trend that American officials hoped would only intensify after the conclusion of fighting. As U.S. soldiers both Caucasians and Indians battled against a common enemy. In addition, Indians joined members of the white workforce on the home front to meet the country's wartime manufacturing needs.

From the vantage point of the Cherokee and their Indian counterparts, though, such experiences exemplified both the advantages and disadvantages of actively participating in the white man's world. On the one hand assimilating into this culture seemed to promise enhanced educational and career opportunities and an overall higher standard of living. Alternately, it meant forfeiting tribal identity, which many Cherokee were unwilling to do.

The Indian Claims Commission Act, which was passed in 1946, was viewed by both whites and Indians as a means to move further toward each group's goals. The legislation allowed Indians to sue the U.S. government over what they considered to be the illegal transfer of tribal lands.

During World War II many American Indians proudly served in the military.

World War II Warriors

While official statistics regarding the number of Cherokee who participated in World War II do not exist, much can be said for the contribution of American Indians as a whole during that conflict. More than 44,000 American Indians served in the U.S. military from 1941 to 1945, including 800 women. In addition, about 20 percent of the American-Indian population claimed roles in the military or was involved in war efforts at home. Six American Indians earned the Congressional Medal of Honor for their efforts during World War II, and Ira Hayes, a Pima Indian from Arizona, was one of six marines to raise the flag on Mount Suribachi in Iwo Jima, Japan.

White politicians were optimistic that the act would resolve tribal complaints of unfair treatment once and for all and would bring Indians that much closer to integrating into mainstream American culture. The Cherokee and other Indian groups assumed a different perspective. They saw a chance to reclaim territory that had been unjustly taken away.

Ultimately, various tribes received more than $800 million in compensation, with the Cherokee gaining $15 million for the forced sale of the Cherokee Outlet. However, they did not recover their land. American officials were more interested in pacifying the Indians and essentially washing their hands of federal responsibility for them and what they perceived to be an endless string of complaints about unfair treatment regarding land, treaties, and rights to self-government. Politicians did not openly regard the act as a strategy for abandonment. On the contrary, they were determined that the Cherokee and other Indians should intermingle with American society, which was experiencing a surge in national unity on the heels of World War II. Officials who approved the act in the 1940s were eager for American Indians to set aside their ties to the past and their cultural identity to assume primary roles as U.S. citizens.

An Extraordinary Ability to Continue Moving Forward

The Cherokee were hesitant to express their desire to pursue goals different from those espoused by the American government. During the 1940s Principal Chief Jesse

B. Milam was especially dedicated to restoring the tribe to its former state of self-government and economic viability. He and several of the principal chiefs who followed in his footsteps pushed to establish businesses such as gaming operations and a return to a stronger political infrastructure within the Cherokee community.

The efforts of these Cherokee leaders were only strengthened by the events and general atmosphere of the 1960s. The civil rights movement swept across the nation, with protestors, public speakers, and everyone from average citizens to politicians pushing for greater equality among all races. To this end the year 1968 saw the formation of the American Indian Movement (AIM) to protest the U.S. government's treatment of tribal peoples. The group staged sit-ins, rallies, and marches — both violent and nonviolent — to raise public and political awareness about the challenges that Indians continued to face more than one hundred years after the Trail of Tears had occurred.

Their persistence gradually paid off for many tribes, including the Cherokee. People of all ethnic backgrounds began to realize the cultural value of New Echota, which was restored and opened to the public as a historic site during the 1960s. That decade also witnessed the Georgia state legislature repeal all laws that had previously robbed the Cherokee of freedom on their ancestral territories. Various Cherokee historical societies and foundations started to form during this era that aimed to repurchase land from the U.S. government and erect museums and preservation sites to commemorate tribal heritage.

A founding member of the American Indian Movement, Russell Means, speaks at a rally.

It appeared that, for the first time in more than a century, the Cherokee and tribes across the country were beginning to gain national recognition as independent and vibrant cultures. During the 1970s American politicians especially started to realize that Indians deserved the same basic rights as U.S. citizens *and* the ability to self-govern to an extent that would enable them to preserve their heritage. In 1971 the Cherokee were therefore allowed to elect their own principal chiefs once more. Four years later they were permitted to practice the same democratic process in appointing members of their tribal council—a right that they had been denied since Oklahoma became a U.S. state.

In addition, 1975 saw the passage in Congress of the Indian Self-Determination and Education Assistance Act, which was created to

> provide maximum Indian participation
> in the government and education of the
> Indian people; to provide for the full
> participation of Indian tribes in programs
> and services conducted by the federal
> government for Indians and to encourage
> the development of human resources of
> the Indian people; to establish a program
> of assistance to upgrade Indian education;
> to support the right of Indian citizens to
> control their own educational activities;
> and for other purposes.

Put more simply, several tribes, including the Cherokee, gained the right to control federal programs and develop programs of their own design. The renewed voice and spirit they subsequently found in self-government allowed them to improve tribal housing, health care, education, and land management.

The Cherokee Nation subsequently ratified a new tribal constitution in 1976 and reclaimed several government buildings in Tahlequah—including the capitol, various courts, and a prison—in the years that followed. In 1983 Wilma P. Mankiller became the Cherokee Nation's first woman to be elected a deputy chief. She was voted the tribe's first female principal chief four years later.

During her tenure as a Cherokee leader Mankiller noted,

> I think that in order to understand the
> contemporary issues we're dealing with
> today and how we plan to dig our way out
> and how indeed we are digging our way
> out, you have to understand a little bit
> about history. Because there are a whole
> lot of historical factors that have played a
> part in our being where we are today, and
> I think that, to even begin to understand
> our contemporary issues and contemporary
> problems, you have to understand a little bit
> about that history.

While few would likely deny the truth behind Mankiller's assessment, questions remain about how modern

A Well-Kept Secret

How has the Cherokee Nation managed to survive the countless hardships it has endured over the last several centuries? "We are a revitalized tribe," Mankiller once famously asserted. "After every major upheaval, we have been able to gather together as a people and rebuild a community and a government. Individually and collectively, Cherokee people possess an extraordinary ability to face down adversity and continue moving forward. We are able to do that because our culture, though certainly diminished, has sustained us since time immemorial. This Cherokee culture is a well-kept secret."

Wilma Mankiller served as principal chief of the Cherokee Nation from 1987 to 1995.

generations of both Caucasians and American Indians recollect and perceive the Trail of Tears nearly two centuries after it occurred. How do present-day perspectives shape a historical event that forever impacted thousands of lives and the relationship between two nations?

Six

A History
Lesson or
a Living
Legacy?

As Mankiller noted during the final decades of the
twentieth century, her people were in the middle of a revitalization that spanned several cultural, economic, and
governmental fronts. The early 1990s saw the Cherokee
Nation signing self-governance agreements with the United
States of America that authorized the tribe to assume responsibility for BIA funds that U.S. officials had previously been
spending on the Cherokees' behalf. This move allowed the
Cherokee Nation to distribute resources and monetary assistance to its community members as it deemed fit, as opposed
to leaving such decisions up to outside agents who weren't as
familiar with tribal needs in such areas as health care, housing, and education.

The late twentieth century was also an era in which
members of the Cherokee Nation returned to their cultural
roots. Those leaders who followed in Mankiller's footsteps in
the mid–1990s spoke both Cherokee and English — marking
the first time in hundreds of years that officials who occupied
such high-ranking positions were full-blooded American
Indians with bilingual capabilities.

By the dawn of the twenty-first century an estimated 10,000 to 15,000 Cherokee spoke their native tongue fluently, and their history and language are currently taught in tribal schools. By 2000 the Cherokee Nation also comprised a massive economic force within Oklahoma, serving as the largest employer in the northeastern part of that state and bolstering the region's economy with roughly $500 million in revenue. Members of the Cherokee Nation are doctors, attorneys, and educators, but the tribe also

The native languages of many American Indians are being taught in tribal schools as a way to keep them from dying out.

contains working-class men and women who face many of the same struggles as people of any ethnicity who reside in the United States.

While the Cherokee have adopted several of the cultural practices prevalent in mainstream American society, they also cherish their own heritage and have taken steps to preserve it for centuries to come. They have regular interactions with government leaders in both Oklahoma and Washington, D.C., and engage in business dealings with U.S. citizens of all races.

As several principal chiefs look on, President George W. Bush signs the Native American Ownership Act in 2007.

An Era of Apologies

Since 2000 the U.S. government has issued apologies to scores of ethnic groups that it admits suffered wrongdoing at its hands. Congress has expressed its sorrow at subjecting African Americans to the injustices of segregation and has voiced the same sentiments to Japanese Americans who were held in internment camps during World War II. As of 2007 that same government body even introduced a bill, which is still being considered, that would offer a similar apology to American Indians. S.J.RES.4 is a joint resolution that proposes to "acknowledge a long history of official depredations and ill-conceived policies by the United States Government regarding Indian tribes and offer an apology to all Native Peoples on behalf of the United States."

People ranging from politicians to university heads have already echoed these concessions to American Indians across the country, but the question remains whether a simple "I'm sorry" is enough to compensate for the thousands of lives that were lost during episodes such as the Trail of Tears, not to mention the hundreds of thousands more that were forever changed in the aftermath. Those individuals responsible for organizing the Day of Remembrance in Murphy, North Carolina, on May 30, 2008, were confident that such an expression of penitence was at least a start. The event was held to commemorate the 170th anniversary of the Trail of Tears and included members of the Cherokee Nation, U.S. congressmen, and religious leaders from across the globe.

"Today is the beginning of the end of an atrocity done many years ago," South African pastor Andre Vaynol stated

A People of the Future

In 2007 the population of the Cherokee Nation was approximately 280,000 individuals—more than seventeen times what it was in the early 1800s. Such statistics seem to go hand in hand with the optimistic outlook of current principal chief Chad Smith, who was quoted as saying in 2004, "We're not only people of the past; we're people of the present, and we're going to be a people of the future."

in conjunction with the Day of Remembrance. "The Trail of Tears should not be a memory of something that is atrocious. It should be a memory of something that was atrocious, but [something that] we overcame." Congressmen who were present reiterated Vaynol's observations.

"Andrew Jackson was wrong," said U.S. Representative Zach Wamp of Tennessee, who is also of Cherokee descent. "People should apologize for the wrongs of the past and make peace one with another." A cornerstone of Wamp's philosophy is ensuring that the past is never forgotten—an effort that the Cherokee Nation has undertaken in full force since the 1980s. For example, the Cherokee Memorial Monument in New Echota was rededicated in 1988 to "keep the memory of the Cherokee's triumphs and struggles alive in [the] hopes that such injustices will never be repeated."

Despite these measures made by some, tensions remain between members of the Cherokee Nation and U.S. officials and flare up from time to time. Racism occurs among all ethnicities, and misconceptions and prejudices exist on the part of both American Indians and individuals who claim other heritage. Factions of non–American Indians resent funding that the U.S. government grants to various tribes and have even suggested to Congress that this aid be cut or reduced. Conversely, certain American Indians will always find it difficult to forget the hardships that they or their ancestors endured at the hands of U.S. administrators. Such memories are deep-rooted and make it difficult to embrace a new generation of politicians and social and religious leaders who are eager to craft whatever amends can realistically be made.

Naturally, the aforementioned challenges and strides toward progress are not merely experienced between heads of state and principal chiefs. They also exist on a universal level—among students, educators, and average citizens whose only connection to the Trail of Tears is often a history book or a long-gone ancestor who traveled west of the Mississippi in 1838. What perspectives do these men and women have on this historic event, and what are their thoughts about ensuring that history never comes close to repeating itself?

Perspectives of the Past

"I am a descendant of two families that endured the immigration," explains Tonia Weavel, a member of the Cherokee Nation and the education director of the Cherokee Heritage Center in Tahlequah. "I do not know specific accounts of any particular family member, but I do know my people lived in northern Georgia before the removal. I often talk about the Trail of Tears and guide school groups through the dedicated exhibit here [at the Cherokee Heritage Center]."

Besides her work as an educator, Weavel believes there are several simple measures that individuals of all ethnic backgrounds can take to prevent any violations of culture similar to the Trail of Tears from occurring in the future. "Basic human respect for a culture different than your own is a very good start," she notes.

> Currently there are thirty-nine federally recognized tribes in the state of Oklahoma, and each of those groups is different in some way from the other. When looking at

the tragic removal period of the Cherokee
people, it is important to know [from a
modern perspective] that the people and
their way of life, the land they live upon,
their customs, language, and dress are all to
be accepted and respected. [For example],
the movie *Dances with Wolves* showed native
people with emotions—humor, anger,
confusion, clarity, and purpose—and marked
one of the first times in our lives where we
were portrayed as real people.

As for Weavel's personal perspective on the Trail of Tears
and its impact on her own life, she adds,

I have never participated in commemoration events related to Indian rights or
remembrances of tragic historical events.
I don't feel a need to relive or carry a chip
on my shoulder about things I cannot change
. . . . My thoughts on the Trail of Tears are
that it is a part of our history . . . from time
immemorial . . . and does not define who we
are then or today. We are much, much more
than victims of the federal government's
hunger for land. We are people still living a
Cherokee life by perpetuating the success
of our families, living comfortably, being
satisfied by having what we need—not what
we want—enjoying games and traditions that

have endured for centuries, living a good
life helping our neighbors and family, and
sleeping with a clear conscience. I, like many
mothers before me, tuck my children into
bed and pat their backs, thankful.

Conversely, Dave Cupp, assistant professor at the University of North Carolina in Chapel Hill, and Dr. Cecilia Minden, a literacy consultant in Chapel Hill, are a married couple who take pride in having participated in reenactments of the Trail of Tears. Cupp and Minden, who claim no American-Indian ancestry, previously lived in Oklahoma and performed in annual dramatizations in Tahlequah that commemorated the events that shaped the Cherokee Nation in 1838 and 1839.

"American Indians became real people [for me] and not merely something from history books," says Cupp of his time in Oklahoma and his contributions to local reenactments of the Trail of Tears. "[This event] needs to be explained not as some aberrant behavior by distant people, but as . . . the long-reaching effects of their decisions. It needs to be taught . . . by people just like us, and not someone from a distant past without any connection to our current lives."

Regardless of the different methods that modern-day citizens of both the United States and the Cherokee Nation use to remember and learn from the Trail of Tears, it is forever embedded in national monuments, history books, novels, films, artwork, and songs. "The Never-Ending Trail" is a poem that was composed by author and songwriter Del "Abe" Jones. The final stanzas of Jones's piece, though

Theater That Does More Than Entertain

The theater is one outlet through which modern-day citizens continue to remember what the Cherokee endured along the Trail of Tears. Since 1969 the Cherokee National Historical Society has sponsored *The Trail of Tears*, an annual outdoor summer drama performed in Tahlequah. Unsurprisingly, the goal of the production reaches far beyond entertaining audiences. In 1977 Martin Hagerstrand, who was then the producer of the play and the executive vice president of the historical society, was quoted as saying, "We were interested in creating a drama which would foster better understanding among Indians and non-Indians alike."

reflective of the element of tragedy that defined the Trail of Tears, also emphasize that the magnitude of this event still resounds within the twenty-first century.

> Each mile of this infamous "Trail"
> Marks the graves of four who died —
> Four thousand poor souls in all
> Marks the shame we try to hide —

A Cherokee prays in front of the U.S. Capitol before the 2004 grand opening of the Smithsonian's National Museum of the American Indian.

You still can hear them crying
Along "The Trail Of Tears"
If you listen with your heart
And not with just your ears.

Yet modern generations are still able to hear much more than the tears of the Cherokee Nation. American Indians and whites alike continue to witness and recognize two hundred years of hardship and pain that have been intermingled with revitalization and success. They acknowledge boundaries between two separate cultures that periodically overlap and maintain similar perspectives on some issues, yet vastly different ones on others. Whether such individuals choose to regard the Trail of Tears as a distant episode in history or a vital force that defines a people's present-day heritage, few can deny that it will live on in both hearts and minds for centuries to come.

Timeline

Mid–1500s   Spanish conquistador Hernando de Soto crosses into Cherokee territory in his pursuit of gold; the tribe first comes into contact with European explorers.

1711–1713   The Cherokee side with the colonists in battle against other tribes in an attempt to maintain control of their territory.

1754–1763   The Cherokee ally themselves with British-American forces during the French and Indian War.

1776–1783   The Cherokee side with the British during the Revolutionary War; they lose 10,000 square miles of land.

Late 1780s   The U.S. Constitution grants Congress and the president exclusive control over Indian affairs.

1802   The U.S. government promises the state of Georgia that it will eliminate any Indian land titles within Georgia's boundaries. It also assures the Cherokee that they need not fear any further reduction of their territory.

1803   The Louisiana Purchase nearly doubles the size of the nation.

Early 1800s   The Cherokee population has dwindled to about 16,000, down from about 30,000 prior to European contact.

1813   The Cherokee side with American forces during the Creek War.

Early 1820s   Sequoyah establishes a written alphabet for the Cherokee language.

1824   American officials establish the Bureau of Indian Affairs (BIA) to oversee all matters related to Indian land management and relations.

Mid–1820s   The Cherokee develop a constitution that provides for a two-body legislature, a court system, and a head chief to lead what the U.S. government comes to acknowledge as the sovereign Cherokee Nation. The tribe declares its capital to be New Echota, in Georgia.

1823   The Cherokee vow to cede no more land to U.S. citizens.

1829   Gold is discovered near Dahlonega, Georgia.

Late 1820s   Georgia politicians consider legislation that will annex Cherokee territories to the state and prohibit anyone of Indian descent from giving testimony in trials that involve white defendants.

May 28, 1830   The Indian Removal Act is signed into law.

Early 1832   John Marshall, chief justice of the U.S. Supreme Court, reaffirms the sovereignty of the Cherokee Nation and its land rights in the southeastern United States; President Andrew Jackson challenges him to enforce his ruling.

1832–1835   The Treaty Party and the National Party become increasingly divided, with each group holding its own council meetings and approaching U.S. officials with distinct policy proposals.

December 29, 1835   The Treaty Party signs the Treaty of New Echota, effectively ceding all Cherokee lands in the southeastern United States to the U.S. government.

Early 1837   A small detachment of Cherokee depart for Indian Territory; greater numbers will follow in the spring of 1838.

May 1838–March 1839   U.S. forces under the command of General Winfield Scott collect and remove between 14,000 and 14,500 Cherokee from their homes. Approximately four thousand die.

June 22, 1839   Tensions escalate between Cherokee political factions in Indian Territory. A new constitution is passed that makes strides toward unifying the tribe.

1844   *The Cherokee Advocate* is published.

1861–1865   The Civil War rages; the majority of the Cherokee support the Confederacy.

1866–1868   Treaties free the Cherokees' slaves and further reduce the tribe's land holdings.

1887   The Dawes Act is signed into law, mandating that tribal properties be allotted to private individuals. The Five Civilized Tribes remain temporarily exempt from allotment, though the Cherokee agree to it in 1905.

September 1893   About 100,000 settlers are permitted to stake property claims in the Cherokee Strip.

1898   The Curtis Act is passed, abolishing all tribal courts and placing all residents of Indian Territory—white or Indian—under federal jurisdiction.

1907   The U.S. government assumes responsibility for appointing the principal chief of the Cherokee Nation; Oklahoma is admitted to the Union as a state; the Cherokee are declared U.S. citizens

1934   The Indian Reorganization Act is passed, reversing many effects of the Dawes Act.

1941–1945   More than 44,000 American Indians serve in the U.S. military during World War II.

1946   The Indian Claims Commission Act is passed, allowing Indians to sue the U.S. government over illegal transfers of tribal lands.

1960s   The civil rights movement sweeps the nation, with supporters pushing for greater equality among all races.

1968   The American Indian Movement (AIM) is created to protest the U.S. government's treatment of tribal peoples.

1970s   Significant self-governing powers are restored to the Cherokee Nation; the Cherokee ratify a new constitution in 1976 and reclaim several government buildings in Tahlequah.

1975   Congress passes the Indian Self-Determination and Education Assistance Act, granting the Cherokee and other tribes greater control over federal programs developed by the Bureau of Indian Affairs.

1983   Wilma P. Mankiller becomes the Cherokee Nation's first woman to be elected a deputy chief. She is voted the tribe's first female principal chief four years later.

1990s   The Cherokee Nation signs agreements with the United States granting tribe members more authority over the distribution of BIA funds.

2000 An estimated 10,000 to 15,000 Cherokee speak fluently in their native tongue by the dawn of the twenty-first century.

2007 Congress considers S.J.RES.4, a joint resolution that proposes a formal apology be made on behalf of the U.S. government to the country's American-Indian population.

May 30, 2008 A Day of Remembrance is held in Murphy, North Carolina, to commemorate the 170th anniversary of the Trail of Tears.

Notes

Chapter One

p. 9, "the trail where they cried": About North Georgia, "The Trail of Tears," http://ngeorgia.com/history/nghisttt.html (accessed August 25, 2008).

p. 10, "O what a year it has been. O what a sweeping wind . . .": Daniel Sabine Butrick, "A Year of Spiritual Darkness," *Voices from the Trail of Tears*, Vicki Rozema, ed. (Winston-Salem, NC: John F. Blair, 2003), pp. 147–148.

p. 11, "principal people": Thomas, Nancy, "Ani'Yun'wiya (The 'Principal People') Legends before and after," The People's Paths, http://www.thepeoplespaths.net/history/AniYunwiya.htm (accessed August 25, 2008).

p. 16, "that these new come Indians be in no sort suffered to seat . . .": English colonist, quoted in "Initial Contacts with the English Colonists," History of the Cherokee, http://cherokeehistory.com/initialc.html (accessed August 25, 2008).

p. 17, "We had hoped the white man would not be willing . . .": Dragging Canoe, quoted in "The Chickamauga: Where Now Are Our Grandfathers, the Delaware?" History of the Cherokee. http://cherokeehistory.com/chickama.html (accessed August 25 2008).

p. 20, "That the Cherokee nation may be led to a greater degree of civilization . . .": The Treaty of Holston, reprinted in "The Cherokees and U.S. Indian Policy," in *The Cherokee Removal: A Brief History with Documents*, Theda Perdue and Michael D. Green, eds. (Boston and New York: Bedford Books of St. Martin's Press, 1995), p. 11.

p. 25, "fixed and unalterable determination never again to cede one foot more of land.": Cherokee Council, quoted in "Political Apprenticeship," in *John Ross, Cherokee Chief*, by Gary E. Moulton. (Athens: University of Georgia Press, 1978), p. 25.

Chapter Two

p. 26, "Philanthropy could not wish to see this continent restored . . .": Andrew Jackson, "President Andrew Jackson's Case for the Removal Act," in *First Annual Message to Congress, 8 December 1830*. Mount Holyoke College: International Relations Program. http://www.mtholyoke.edu/acad/intrel/andrew.htm (accessed August 25, 2008).

p. 31, "an act to provide for an exchange of lands . . .": The Indian Removal Act, "Twenty-First Congress, Session One, Chapter 148, 1830" in *A Century of Lawmaking for a New Nation: U.S. Congressional Documents and Debates, 1774–1875*. The Library of Congress: American Memory. http://memory.loc.gov/cgi-bin/ampage?collId=llsl&fileName=004/llsl004.db&recNum=458 (accessed August 25, 2008).

p. 32, "Our children by thousands yearly leave the land . . .": Andrew Jackson, "President Andrew Jackson's Case for the Removal Act," in *First Annual Message to Congress, 8 December 1830*.

p. 33, "The evil. . . .is enormous . . .": Edward Everett, "Speeches on the Passage of the Bill for the Removal of the Indians Delivered in the Congress of the United States," in *Statements from the Debate on Indian Removal.* Columbia University. http://www.columbia.edu/~lmg21/BC3180/removal.html (accessed August 25, 2008).

p. 34, "If the country to which we go is so desirable . . .": Major Ridge, "Introduction," in *Voices from the Trail of Tears*, p. 14.

p. 34, "The citizens of Georgia have no right to enter . . .": John Marshall, "Georgia Policy," in *The Cherokee Removal*, 1995, p. 74.

p. 37, "The Cherokee Nation hereby cede, relinquish, and convey to the United States . . .": Treaty of New Echota, "Article One," *Treaty with the Cherokee, 1835.* Oklahoma State University Library: Indian Affairs: Laws and Treaties. http://digital.library.okstate.edu/KAPPLER/VOL2/treaties/che0439.htm#mn2 (accessed August 25, 2008).

p. 38, ". . . express the sorrowful conviction that it is impossible . . .": 1834 Resolution of the Treaty Party, "Introduction," in *Voices from the Trail of Tears*, p. 15.

p. 39, "I have signed my death warrant.": Major Ridge, quoted in "The Cherokee Phoenix and American Indian Intellectual History," *Multicultural Studies in the American South*, The University of Georgia. http://www.uga.edu/msis/weavertext.html (accessed August 25, 2008).

p. 39, "Many have said they will die before they leave the country.": John E. Wool, "Introduction," in *Voices from the Trail of Tears*, p. 15.

p. 42, "My troops already occupy many positions in the country that you are to abandon . . .": Winfield Scott, "Letter to the Cherokee from Major General Scott," *Cultural Information: The Trail of Tears*. The Official Site of the Cherokee Nation. http://www.cherokee.org/Culture/CulInfo/TOT/125/Default.aspx (accessed August 25, 2008).

p. 44, "It is spring. The leaves are on the trees. . . .": Samuel Cloud (as relayed by Michael Rutledge), quoted in "Samuel's Memory" History of the Cherokee. http://cherokeehistory.com/samuel.html (accessed August 25, 2008).

p. 46, "I saw the helpless Cherokees arrested and dragged from their homes . . .": John G. Burnett, "Birthday Story of Private John G. Burnett, Captain Abraham McClellan's Company, Second Regiment, Second Brigade, Mounted Infantry, Cherokee Indian Removal, 1838–39." *John G. Burnett's Story of the Removal of the Cherokees*. Powersource. http://www.powersource.com/cherokee/burnett.html (accessed August 25, 2008).

Chapter Three

p. 48, "I experienced no difficulty in getting them to move along . . .": L. B. Webster, "Introduction," in *Voices from the Trail of Tears*, p. 28.

p. 49, "The troops and Indians, in all their camps": Winfield Scott, "Introduction," in *Voices from the Trail of Tears*, p. 29.

p. 51, ". . . writes that the Cherokee were suffering severely . . .":
the *Missionary Herald*, "Introduction," in *Voices from the Trail of Tears*, p. 29.

p. 53, "The people got so tired of eating salt[ed] pork . . .":
Rebecca Neugin, "Introduction," in *Voices from the Trail of Tears*, p. 31.

p. 54, "A great many ride on horseback, and multitudes go . . .":
traveler from Maine in the *New York Observer*, quoted in
"Introduction," in *Voices from the Trail of Tears*, p. 34.

p. 56, "Every possible kindness, compatible with the necessity
of removal must . . .": Winfield Scott, "Appendix Two:
General Winfield Scott's Removal Order Number 25,"
in *Voices from the Trail of Tears*, pp. 196–197.

p. 57, "I have through the Civil War and have seen men
shot . . .": Georgia militiaman who participated in the
"roundup" of the Cherokee Indians, "Quotations," *Trail of
Tears*. Cerritos College: American Identities. http://www.
cerritos.edu/soliver/American%20Identities/Trail%20
of%20Tears/quotes.htm (accessed August 26, 2008).

p. 58, "Very few of the Indians had been able to bring . . .":
an elderly Cherokee woman, quoted in "Stalemate and
Terrorism, 1841–1846," in *After the Trail of Tears: The Cherokees'
Struggle for Sovereignty*, William G. McLoughlin. (Chapel Hill:
University of North Carolina Press), 1993, p. 35.

p. 59, "The ancient customs of the nation are all gone.": Ethan
Allen Hitchcock, "The Trail of Tears," in *The Cherokee
Removal*, 1995, p. 171.

p. 59, "As we approached Tahlequa, we met . . .": Hitchcock, "The Trail of Tears," in *The Cherokee Removal*, p. 172.

Chapter Four

p. 62, "Beyond the great River Mississippi, where a part of your nation has gone . . .": Andrew Jackson, "The Rape of the Native American People," in *Disasters*. Boise State University. http://www.boisestate.edu/history/ncasner/hy210/tears.htm (accessed August 26, 2008).

p. 63, "The peculiar circumstances of their condition admonish the Cherokees . . .": John Ross, "Neutrality and the Alliance with the Confederate States of America," History of the Cherokee. http://cherokeehistory.com/Ross_Proclamation_for_Neutrality_05_17_1861.htm (accessed August 26, 2008).

p. 73, "Let lay side his picturesque blankets . . .": Philip Garret, in "The End of Sovereignty, 1880–1907," in *After the Trail of Tears*, p. 369.

p. 74, "I have always believed that the Great Creator . . .": Redbird Smith, "Bits of Ani'Yun'wiya History," *Notable Cherokee Quotes*. The People's Paths. http://www.thepeoplespaths.net/Cherokee/QuotesOfCherokees.htm (accessed August 26, 2008).

Chapter Five

p. 80, "The main thing now is that at least they have a will to live. ": John Collier, "Indian Fighter," *Time*,

February 19, 1945, http://www.time.com/time/magazine/
article/0,9171,778328,00.html (accessed August 26, 2008).

p. 81, ". . . provide maximum Indian participation in the
government and education . . .": The Indian Self-
Determination and Education Assistance Act, "S.1017,"
Bills, Resolutions. The Library of Congress. http://thomas.
loc.gov/cgi-bin/bdquery/z?d093:SN01017:TOM:/bss/
d093query.html (accessed August 26, 2008).

p. 88, "I think that in order to understand the contemporary
issues . . .": Wilma P. Mankiller, "Speech By Wilma
P. Mankiller, Former Chief, Cherokee Nation, OK," in
Rebuilding the Cherokee Nation. The People's Paths. http://
www.thepeoplespaths.net/articles/Mankiller930402
RebuildingCNO.htm (accessed August 26, 2008).

p. 89, "We are a revitalized tribe . . .": Wilma P. Mankiller,
"Wilma Mankiller, Former Principal Chief of the
Cherokee Nation. *Gallery.* 1996. Powersource. http://www.
powersource.com/gallery/people/wilma.html (accessed
August 26, 2008).

Chapter Six

p. 95, ". . . acknowledge a long history of official depredations
. . .": "S.J.RES.4," *Bills, Resolutions.* The Library of
Congress, http://thomas.loc.gov/cgi-bin/bdquery/
z?d109:SJ00004 (accessed August 26, 2008).

p. 95, "Today is the beginning of the end of an atrocity . . .":
Andre Vaynol, in "Christians Remember Trail of Tears,"

Charisma Magazine, August 2008, http://www.charisma
mag.com/display.php?id=17488 (accessed August 26,
2008).

p. 96, "We're not people of the past, we're people of the
present . . .": Chad Smith, "History Unseen," CNN.com
September 21, 2004, http://www.cnn.com/2004/US/09/21/
history.unseen/ (accessed August 26, 2008).

p. 97, "Andrew Jackson was wrong . . .": Zach Wamp, in
"Christians Remember Trail of Tears."

p. 97, ". . . keep the memory of the Cherokees' triumphs
and struggles alive . . .": rededication on the Cherokee
Memorial Monument at New Echota, "1988," Cherokee
History Timeline. Cherokee Bill's Trade Center. http://
wsharing.org/WScherokeeTimeline.htm (accessed August
26, 2008).

p. 98, "I am a descendant of two families that endured the
immigration . . .": Interview with Tonia Weavel, education
director, Cherokee Heritage Center, August 14, 2008.

p. 98, "Basic human respect for a culture different than your
own. . . .": Interview with Tonia Weavel.

p. 99, "I have never participated in commemoration events . . ."
Interview with Tonia Weavel.

p. 100, "American Indians became real people [for me] . . .":
Interview with Dave Cupp, assistant professor, the
University of North Carolina in Chapel Hill, August 20,
2008.

p. 101, "We were interested in creating a drama. . .": Martin
Hagerstrand, "Fact and Fiction: The Trail of Tears,"

Journal of American Indian Education. Arizona State University: Mary Lou Fulton College of Education. http://jaie.asu.edu/v16/V16S2fac.html (accessed August 27, 2008).

p. 102, "The Never-Ending Trail," Del "Abe" Jones, in The Trail of Tears. About North Georgia, http://ngeorgia.com/poetry/theneverendingtrail.html (accessed August 26, 2008).

Further Information

Books

Bowes, John P. *The Trail of Tears: Removal in the South*. New York: Chelsea House, 2007.

Royce, Charles C. *The Cherokee Nation*. New Brunswick, NJ: Aldine Transaction, 2007.

Rozema, Vicki, ed. *Voices from the Trail of Tears*. Winston-Salem, NC: John F. Blair, 2003.

Sturgis, Amy H. *The Trail of Tears and Indian Removal*. Westport, CT: Greenwood Press, 2007.

DVD

The Trail of Tears: Cherokee Legacy. Rich-Heape Films, Inc., 2006.

Websites

History of the Cherokee

http://cherokeehistory.com

A collection of primary and secondary resources related to the history and culture of the tribe.

The Official Site of the Cherokee Nation

http://www.cherokee.org

An overview of both current and historical issues related to the Cherokee Nation.

Bibliography

Books

Ehle, John. *Trail of Tears: The Rise and Fall of the Cherokee Nation*. New York: Anchor Books: Doubleday, 1988.

Jahoda, Gloria. *The Trail of Tears*. New York: Wings Books, 1975.

McLoughlin, William G. *After the Trail of Tears: The Cherokees' Struggle for Sovereignty, 1839–1880*. Chapel Hill: University of North Carolina Press, 1993.

Moulton, Gary E. *John Ross, Cherokee Chief*. Athens: University of Georgia Press, 1978.

Perdue, Theda, and Michael D. Green, eds. *The Cherokee Nation and the Trail of Tears*. New York: Viking, 2007.

———. *The Cherokee Removal: A Brief History with Documents*. Boston: Bedford Books of St. Martin's Press, 2005.

Royce, Charles C. *The Cherokee Nation*. New Brunswick, NJ: Aldine Transaction, 2007.

Rozema, Vicki, ed. *Voices from the Trail of Tears*. Winston-Salem, NC: John F. Blair, 2003.

Sturgis, Amy H. *The Trail of Tears and Indian Removal*. Westport, CT: Greenwood Press, 2007.

Interviews

Interview with Dave Cupp, assistant professor, the University of North Carolina in Chapel Hill, August 20, 2008.

Interview with Cecilia Minden, literacy consultant in Chapel Hill, North Carolina, August 20, 2008.

Interview with Tonia Weavel, education director, Cherokee Heritage Center, August 14, 2008.

Websites

About North Georgia
http://ngeorgia.com

Journal of American Indian Education — Arizona State University
"Fact and Fiction: The Trail of Tears"
http://jaie.asu.edu/v16/V16S2fac.html

Boise State University
"Trail of Tears: The Rape of the Native American People"
http://www.boisestate.edu/history/ncasner/hy210/tears.htm

Cerritos College — American Identities
"Quotations: Trail of Tears"
http://www.cerritos.edu/soliver/American%20IdentitiesTrail%20of%20Tears/quotes.htm

Charisma Magazine
"Christians Remember Trail of Tears"
http://www.charismamag.com/display.php?id=17488

Cherokee History Timeline
http://wsharing.org/WScherokeeTimeline.htm

CNN.com
"History Unseen?"
http://www.cnn.com/2004/US/09/21/history.unseen/

Columbia University
http://www.columbia.edu/~lmg21/BC3180/removal.html

History of the Cherokee
http://cherokeehistory.com

The Library of Congress — American Memory
http://memory.loc.gov/cgi-bin/ampage?collId=llsl&fileName
=004/llsl004.db&recNum=458

The Library of Congress
http://thomas.loc.gov

Mount Holyoke College — International Relations Program
"President Andrew Jackson's Case for the Removal Act"
http://www.mtholyoke.edu/acad/intrel/andrew.htm

The Official Site of the Cherokee Nation
http://www.cherokee.org

Oklahoma State University — Indian Affairs: Laws and Treaties
http://digital.library.okstate.edu/KAPPLER/VOL2/treaties/
che0439.htm#mn2

The People's Paths
"Rebuilding the Cherokee Nation"
http://www.thepeoplespaths.net

Powersource
"Cherokee Messenger"
http://www.powersource.com

Time Magazine **— February 19, 1945**
"Indian Fighter"
http://www.time.com/time/magazine/article/0,9171,778328,00
.html

The University of Georgia
http://www.uga.edu/msis/weavertext.html

Index

Page numbers in **boldface** are illustrations.

About the Author

KATIE MARSICO is the author of more than forty reference books for children and young adults. Prior to becoming a full-time writer, Marsico worked as a managing editor in publishing. She resides near Chicago, Illinois, with her husband and children.